Avoiding Drugs

by Patricia J Murphy

Series consultants: Sonja Green, MD, and
Distinguished Professor Emerita Ann Nolte, PhD

Lerner Books • London • New York • Minneapolis

For my nephew, Erik (aka Alex), and my niece, Olivia—Love, Auntie Patty

The author would like to thank Mathea Falco, president of Drug Strategies; Dominic Cappello; Robert Schwebel, PhD; and Joel Spivak and Daniel E McGoldrick with the Campaign for Tobacco-Free Kids, as well as countless others for their assistance in the research of this book. In addition, she would like to thank her editor, Catherine Creswell, for her enthusiasm for and support of this project.

This book was first published in the United States of America in 2006.

First published in the United Kingdom in 2008 by
Lerner Books,
Dalton House,
60 Windsor Avenue,
London SW19 2RR

Website address: www.lernerbooks.co.uk

This edition was updated and edited for UK publication by Discovery Books Ltd., Unit 3, 37 Watling Street, Leintwardine, Shropshire SY7 0LW

Words in **bold** type are explained in a glossary on page 31.

British Library Cataloguing in Publication Data

Murphy, Patricia J., 1963-
   Avoiding drugs. - (Pull ahead books. Health)
   1. Drug abuse - Juvenile literature 2. Drug abuse -
   Prevention - Juvenile literature
   I. Title
   613.8

ISBN-13: 978 1 58013 399 9

Printed in China

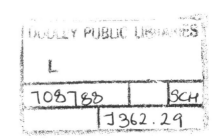

Olivia has a bad cough. Her father gives her cough **medicine.**

Olivia's medicine is an **over-the-counter drug.** It will help stop Olivia's cough.

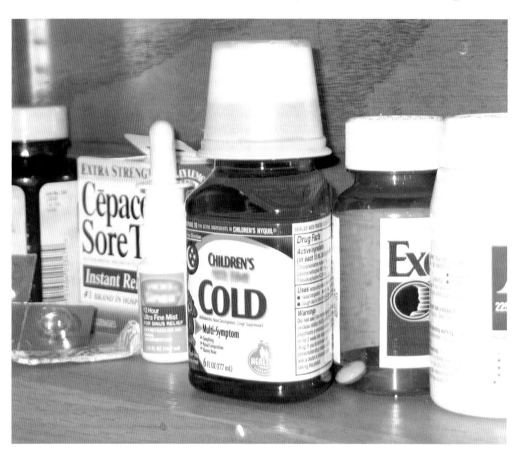

Her father buys it at the shop. What over-the-counter drugs can you find at the shop?

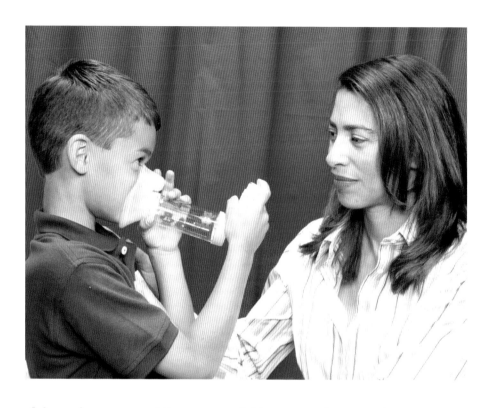

Alex has **asthma**. His mother gives him asthma medicine. Alex's medicine is a **prescription** drug. It will help Alex when he has trouble breathing.

Alex's doctor orders the drug for him.
The medicine is only for Alex. His
mother buys it at the prescription
counter at the chemist.

Olivia and Alex only take medicine their parents or doctors give them. Their parents read and follow the directions.

The right amount of medicine can help them get well. The wrong amount or the wrong medicine could hurt them!

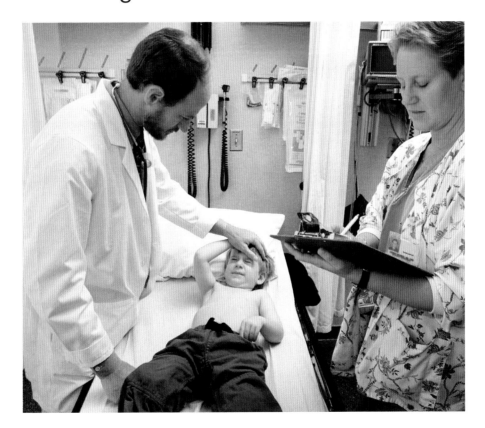

Medicines and vitamins are drugs. Drugs change the way your body works.

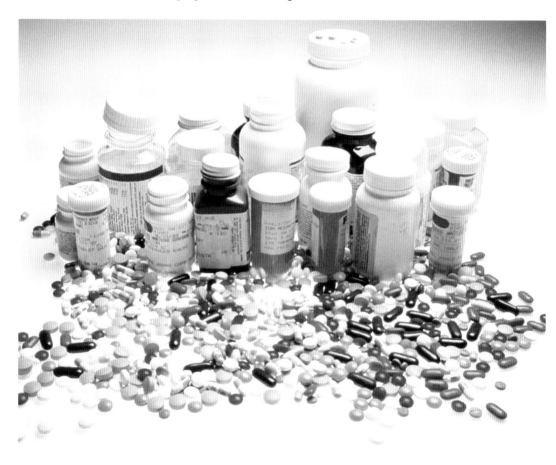

Some drugs help you to stay healthy.
Others help you when you are ill. These
drugs are called **medicinal drugs.**

Some drugs won't help you stay healthy. They may even hurt your body or make you sick. These drugs are called **non-medicinal drugs.**

Alcohol and **nicotine** are non-medicinal drugs. They can be harmful to the body. They may cause illness and even death.

Some people **misuse** these or other drugs. They might take drugs when they feel sad, lonely or bored.

They hope the drugs will change the way they feel. But often the drugs make them very sick. Sometimes people can't stop using drugs!

Tommy's grandma smokes cigarettes. Most days she coughs a lot. She also has trouble breathing.

Tommy
wonders why
she smokes.
Do you know
why?

Cigarettes are made with **tobacco.**
Tobacco has nicotine in it. It makes it
hard for people to stop smoking.

Tobacco can
cause lung
cancer and
other illnesses.

At parties Sue's aunt always has a drink in her hand. She talks loudly and acts silly. Sometimes she falls over.

Why do you think Sue's aunt acts this way?

Her aunt drinks too much alcohol. Alcohol is in drinks like beer and wine. Alcohol changes how people feel and act.

Drinking too much alcohol makes some people feel sad. It can make others feel angry. Over time, too much alcohol can hurt the body and mind.

Most adults can drink some alcohol and stop. Others, like Sue's aunt, can't stop. They need help!

People who drink alcohol and drive can hurt or kill themselves and others. Drinking and driving is against the law.

It's everyone's job to be smart about drugs. Olivia and Alex only take the drugs their parents and doctors give to them.

Olivia and Alex stay away from non-medicinal drugs. You can too!

What I've Learned

■ Only take medicine your parents, a trusted adult or doctor gives you.

■ The wrong medicine or wrong amount of medicine can hurt you.

■ Some drugs are not medicine. They do not help you stay healthy. Nicotine and alcohol are these kinds of drugs.

■ Nicotine makes it hard to stop smoking.

■ Alcohol can make people feel and act differently. Alcohol makes it hard for some people to stop drinking it.

■ Some people misuse drugs when they feel sad. Sometimes they can't stop using drugs.

■ Drinking and driving is against the law.

Have a Drug-Free Plan

A friend may ask you to try drugs. Learn how to say no. Practise these lines with someone.

Person 1: Do you want to smoke?
Person 2: No, way! I like breathing.

Person 1: Try this drug. It will make you feel great.
Person 2: I like the way I feel. Drugs only make you feel sick!

Person 1: Come on. Have a drink. It'll make you do silly things.
Person 2: No thanks! I like being myself.

Person 1: Try this drug. Everybody's doing it!
Person 2: No, not everyone's doing it – because I'm NOT doing it.

Person 1: If you were my friend, you'd do this drug with me.
Person 2: If you keep doing drugs, I can't be your friend!

Books and Websites

Books

Haughton, Emma. *Drinking, Smoking, and Other Drugs* (Health & Fitness) Raintree, 2000.

Lamb, Kirsten. *Alcohol* (Health Issues) Raintree, 2001.

Medina, Sarah. *Drugs – What's the Danger?* (Get Wise) Heinemann Library, 2005.

Waters, Fiona. *Drugs* (What About Health) Hodder Wayland, 2004.

Westcott, Patsy. *Why Do People Take Drugs?* (Exploring Tough Issues) Raintree, 2001.

Websites

Parents Centre
http://www.parentscentre.gov.uk

Advice for schools and families
http://www.schoolsweb.gov.uk

Advice for young people
http://www.talktofrank.com

Glossary

alcohol: a liquid found in drinks like wine or beer

asthma: a condition that can cause trouble breathing

medicinal drugs: drugs that can keep the body healthy or treat illness

medicine: a drug used to treat an illness

misuse: to use something the wrong way

nicotine: a drug found in tobacco, in cigarettes and cigars

non-medicinal drugs: drugs that affect the body but that do not treat an illness

over-the-counter drug: a drug that can be bought without a doctor's order

prescription: a doctor's order for a drug

tobacco: leaves of the tobacco plant used to make cigarettes and cigars

Index

alcohol 13, 22–25, 28

drinking and driving 25, 28

medicine 3, 4, 6–11, 28

misusing drugs 4–15, 22, 28

nicotine 13, 18, 28

non-medicinal drugs 12–13, 27

over-the-counter drugs 4, 5

prescription drugs 6, 7

proper use of medicine 8–9, 26, 28

saying no to drugs 26, 29

smoking 16–18

tobacco 18, 19, 28

Photo Acknowledgements

The photographs in this book appear with the permission of: © Todd Strand/Independent Picture Service, front cover, pp 3, 4, 6, 7, 8, 16, 17, 18, 20, 21, 22, 23, 26, 27; © Sam Lund/Independent Picture Service, p 5; © Royalty-Free/CORBIS, pp 9, 11, 14; © PhotoDisc/Getty Images, pp 10, 15, 19, 24, 25; © Bobby Humphrey/Discovery Books, pp 12, 13.